CATCH
IMPLEMENTATION GUIDE

Catch: A Churchwide Program for Invitational Evangelism

Program Guide with DVD ROM
Everything needed for the pastor or leadership team to plan the program
978-1-4267-4347-4

Small Group Participant Book
Four-week adult study to get the congregation on board
978-1-4267-4301-6

Small Group DVD with Leader Guide
Inspirational videos for four small group sessions
978-1-4267-4161-6

Implementation Guide
Follow up guide for leadership group or implementation team
978-1-4267-4300-9

Catch Kit
One of each component
843504028459

CATCH

A CHURCHWIDE PROGRAM FOR INVITATIONAL EVANGELISM

Implementation Guide

Debi Nixon

Abingdon Press / Nashville

CATCH: IMPLEMENTATION GUIDE
DEBI NIXON

COPYRIGHT © 2012 BY ABINGDON PRESS
ALL RIGHTS RESERVED.

This book is printed on acid-free, elemental chlorine-free paper.

ISBN: 978-142-674300-9

12 13 14 15 16 17 18 19 20 21 — 10 9 8 7 6 5 4 3 2

MANUFACTURED IN THE UNITED STATES OF AMERICA

Contents

Introduction

The *Catch* approach to invitational evangelism is focused on intentional, step-by-step practices that help you reach outside the walls of your church, attract new people to your church family, and connect those new people into the life of your church. As you take seriously Jesus' instruction to go and fish for people, you will need a tackle box full of tools to attract and connect people to your church. As these people become connected, you will need to employ practices that help them find a path to membership and ultimately become committed disciples of Jesus Christ.

This Implementation Guide is designed for use with the Program Guide (which introduces *Catch* to the pastor and church leaders and helps them organize the program and its worship component). It is also intended for use with the Small Group Participant Book and Small Group DVD with Leader Guide (both of which bring the congregation into the program through Sunday school classes and small groups). Following the congregation-wide worship and small group activities described in these resources, teams of committed church members fan out through the church and community to implement the program, putting the *Catch* approach into practice. This Implementation Guide presents instructions for these teams in a step-by-step format that will be easy to understand and follow, so the teams can energize, organize, and do the good work that will need to be done.

In the pages that follow, you will find four chapters of practices specific to attracting new visitors, hospitality, connecting, and membership. Within the chapters is a general overview of the practices pertaining to that chapter, along with step-by-step instructions with assignable task lists, samples, and reproducible scripts and forms.

Ideally, you will have teams for each of the four chapters. However, the reality of many churches is that there are only so many people to do the work. In such cases, crossover is fine. For example, one team might take hold of all of the practices and employ them one after the other. The most important thing is to make sure someone is championing each effort.

The techniques of invitational evangelism are divided into four categories:

1. Attracting People in Your Community

The concepts of church and marketing may seem like oil and water, and sometimes it may feel that marketing is for the business and secular world only. But all through the Bible we see stories of persuasion, word-of-mouth messaging, and grassroots marketing. By marketing we don't mean stealing members from other churches through a slick campaign or a tech-savvy Web site presence. We mean fishing for people—those people in your community who have never known or have forgotten about God's love and plan for them. The techniques in Chapter 1 will help you reach out to your community and tell the story about who your church is and what you're about.

2. Making Visitors Feel Welcome

If you are going to get serious about marketing your church and attracting people in your community, you will need to take a good look at the level of hospitality those people will encounter when they walk through your doors. This can be a difficult step because it is hard to look objectively at ourselves. We want to believe that we are doing everything we can to make people feel welcome. We think we are friendly enough. We assume people can walk right in and find an entry point to service, worship, and fellowship. However, for most of us there are things we could do better, things we need to stop doing, and new practices we need to take on. The techniques found in Chapter 2 will help you cover every touch point a visitor might experience and make sure that you have thought of everything to create a warm, welcoming, and inviting environment for everyone.

3. Connecting and Following Up With Visitors

You have attracted visitors to your church from your effective marketing methods. You have created a welcoming environment and thought of every way possible to help visitors feel at home when they arrive. The next step is to follow up with them and help them get connected. Ideally, visitors should not attend your church anonymously week after week without finding any point of connection or engagement. The practices in Chapter 3 will give you specific ideas for connecting with visitors as well as a plan to follow up with them.

4. Inviting Others to Grow in Faith

The point of all this effort is to help people become fully committed disciples of Jesus Christ. The steps in this book are meaningless apart from this goal. As you become a church of invitational evangelists, remember that a plan for ongoing discipleship is of utmost importance. Once new people are coming to your church, being welcomed, and getting connected, you need an obvious path to membership and a clear journey of discipleship. The practices in Chapter 4 and the Documents for Ministries and Planning, found in the Appendix, will help you plan to emphasize membership and lead people to love and serve God in Jesus Christ more fully.

• • •

As you embark on this fishing expedition, try to view every aspect of your church through the eyes of a visitor, especially one who has no prior experience in the church. Do everything you can to make your church a place where people gather to love God, serve God, and live in fellowship with other believers. Communicate in every way that all are welcome and loved—that all can have their deepest needs met in the love and grace of Jesus Christ. Do everything you can to invite visitors into the journey of following Jesus—a path that will give them peace, assurance, and joy such as they never have known.

Jesus told his disciples to fish for people. So, cast your nets wide and expect God to fill them to overflowing. Blessings to you as you obey Jesus' call and make every effort to reach people with the amazing love of God in Jesus Christ.

1.
Attracting People in Your Community

1.
Attracting People
in Your Community

I graduated college with a degree in marketing. I spent four years studying how to persuade customers that a particular product or service would be the answer to their needs. During college, my classmates and I learned about the four P's of marketing—product, price, promotion, and place—by examining case studies of effective marketers. For the next decade I used my education to persuade women that well-made, tailored clothing met their need for fashion, sophistication, versatility, and comfort. I loved what I did. I knew that if a woman felt good about what she was wearing, her self-esteem was higher, she felt better about herself, and the quality of her life improved for a season.

When I left the world of retail to join the staff at Church of the Resurrection in Leawood, Kansas, I assumed I would be setting aside what I had learned and practiced in the field of marketing. I never thought a church would use marketing, promotion, and product development techniques; they were so secular, so consumer-driven, or so I thought. I quickly discovered this assumption was wrong. In fact, I discovered the Bible would have been a great source for case studies in our marketing classes.

The goal of marketing is to identify the needs of the customer, provide a product to meet those needs, and generate ways to spread the word so that others know about the product. Jesus was highly effective at marketing. As Jesus encountered people, he identified their needs and met those needs by calling the people to him, and word spread quickly about what he had to offer. Jesus' encounter with a woman at a well, recorded in the Gospel of John, was one example of effective marketing. While in the woman's town, Jesus noticed her and made it a priority to learn more about her. He asked questions and made observations. He identified her need and offered her living water to meet that need. The woman ran to tell her friends about the life-changing "product" she had been given. Word spread quickly.

Many of the Samaritans from the woman's town came to believe in Jesus because of the woman's testimony: "He told me everything I've ever done." When they urged him to stay, Jesus remained in the town for two days. Because of his words, many more became believers. They said to the woman, "We no longer believe just because of what you said, for we have heard for ourselves and know that this one is truly the savior of the world" (John 4:39-42).

Many pastors and church leaders are hesitant to embrace marketing techniques. They say marketing is manipulative, secular, and customer-driven. Technically they are right, but does that make it something to avoid? Let's look at the definitions of these words.

Manipulate: To manage or utilize skillfully

Secular: Of or relating to the worldly or temporal

Customer: An individual usually having some specified distinctive trait

Given these definitions, is marketing still something to avoid in the church? What do we think Jesus would say and do? (WWJD—now, that's marketing.) I believe that Scripture shows over and over again that Jesus managed and utilized his ability to connect with people (customers), providing a response to a worldly or temporal need. And he was convincing.

Marketing involves persuasion. Paul persuaded people to a better way of living. Through marketing, you are persuading non-religious and nominally religious people to consider what the church has to offer. You are seeking to motivate and inspire them to respond on their journey to become followers of Jesus Christ.

Applying the Four P's to Church Marketing

Product refers to the goods or service you have to offer. Our "product" is the good news of Jesus Christ. Jesus is the good news and answer to our deepest human needs. He is what we have to offer.

Price refers to the process of setting a value on the product, and it does not always have to be monetary. We know that our lives were bought and paid for at a large price, but the product we receive is offered freely.

Promotion refers to the various ways of promoting the product. Through promotion you are communicating to people that you have answers to their needs. This is evangelism—promoting the love of God to the world so the world may come to know God's love for them.

Place refers to ways to get the product to the customer. In churches, this includes worship services, the building, and ministry programs. If these are your distribution channels, then how intentionally have you designed ministry programs aimed at reaching the non-religious and nominally religious?

Applying the four P's to your church marketing efforts does not necessarily mean your efforts will bear immediate fruit. Marketers will tell you that it may take up to seven different exposures or contacts before someone will take a next step. Stay committed to your purpose and remain prayerful in all things. You may find helpful the following general advice on developing marketing plans from Peter Metz, Director of Communications at Church of the Resurrection and author of *Marketing Your Church to the Community* (Abingdon Press, 2007).

1. Always think strategically. Start by determining who you want to reach and what is important to them; then, tailor your messages to that audience and speak their language.

2. Keep to a single-minded message. Too often churches put too many things in their communications and nothing comes through clearly.

3. Do only what you can do well. Your communications make a statement about who you are. You never want to do something poorly, so avoid things you can't do well. If you can't do TV or radio well because they require expertise you don't have, don't do them.

4. Remember the importance of personal invitation. Look for tools and ways to empower your members to extend personal invitations. It is the most effective way of getting visitors in your front door. Over nine in ten of our visitors say that personal invitation was the primary reason they visited Resurrection.

Work the Steps

Step 1. Evaluate the Current Marketing Effort and Message

Gather the marketing team and review your current marketing efforts. What mail pieces do you currently send out? Are these for members or people outside your walls? What is your social media presence? As you review your printed marketing materials, where do you think you're doing "pretty well"? What will it take to do everything with excellence? Do you need to eliminate something?

Make a list of everything you do in terms of marketing: Web site, mailings, newspaper ads, radio spots, and so on. Get everything on the table and take a good look at how your church presents itself to the community. Evaluate your marketing messages and efforts based on these questions:

- Does the message speak to people who don't go to church here or people outside our walls?
- Does the message tell people what we want them to know about our church?
- Do the message and design of the piece feel inviting and welcoming?

As you work through the rest of the marketing techniques in this section, decide which of the practices you will start doing and which you will stop doing. Commit to a clear, committed focus on communicating exactly what you want people in your area to know about your church and how it will meet the deepest need they have—to know God's love in Jesus Christ.

Tasks:

- Review all marketing efforts.
- Evaluate your mailings, posters, Web site, and so on with the eyes of a potential visitor.
- Make necessary adjustments to remove old content and replace with new messaging.
- Create or update the Web site with homepage information that is helpful for first-time visitors.
- Evaluate the user-friendliness of your Web site. Is first-time visitor information prominent? (This includes such items as worship service times and locations, event calendar, contact names and information, and links to additional information.) What does your Web site communicate that you value? Invite one to two volunteers who

have experience in Web development to evaluate your site and help implement recommended changes.

- Work with the pastor and worship team to identify a "take-away" item for each person in worship during the *Catch* sermon series—bookmarks, key tags, weekly Scripture reading tool, or other items.

- Assign a team member to create a church Facebook page and Twitter account. Keep the Facebook page updated with current worship and program information. Work with the pastor to create two to three tweets a week, announcing events or sending encouragement to followers.

Step 2. Plan Your Direct Mail

Adam Hamilton writes,

> Direct mail works on the law of large numbers. Your response rate for a well-designed direct mail piece might be only one-tenth of one percent; if you send out three thousand pieces that might indicate that as few as three to as many as ten households would visit. Often the response rate is much higher, but be prepared for a rate within this range."
>
> (*Leading Beyond the Walls*, pp. 36-37)

Begin with Christmas or Easter. A month before the holiday worship services, buy a mailing list of your area and send out postcards inviting people to church and communicating what your pastor will be preaching about.

Beyond Christmas and Easter, create a plan for sending direct mail pieces about new programs, events, and ministries. Plan to send at least four pieces out every year, including the two holiday pieces.

Tasks:

- Brainstorm four to five times a year when you might use a direct mail piece, beginning with Christmas and Easter.
- Determine your target radius.
- Determine how to get a database of household mailing addresses.
- Determine how many direct mail pieces you will print.
- Print additional direct mail pieces in your weekend bulletin as a tool for your members to use when inviting their friends.

- Secure a professional quality designer and copywriter.
- Make sure the design of each piece communicates exactly what you want it to. Ask yourself: Does this message speak to non-religious and nominally religious people, or does it connect only with our own church members? Does the image and feel of the piece make our church appear welcoming and inviting? Don't forget to put the name, address, phone number, and worship times of your church in the direct mail pieces.

Step 3. Create Information Packets and Materials for the Connection Center

When the *Catch* approach to invitational evangelism is in full swing in your church, you will have a connection center in your main lobby where all information about the church can be found, as well as volunteers to staff it. In addition, the pastor or a team of volunteers will deliver mugs or another small gift to first-time visitors each week along with materials about the church and its ministries. Your marketing team is tasked with providing the current materials for the connection center as well as visitor information for the mugging team.

Your team will need to go to every program ministry leader (youth, children, adult, music, women's, men's, and so on) to get updated information about the mission of that ministry, their meeting times, how visitors can find them, and a contact person's name and phone number. Work with the respective ministry leaders to create a brochure, postcard, or flyer that reflects the vision and communicates the excitement of that ministry.

Once you have all the ministry brochures, use them to stock the connection center, and work with the mugging team to make sure they have all the materials they need.

Tasks:

- Assign marketing team members to meet with each ministry leader in the church to plan an updated brochure, postcard, or flyer communicating the purpose of that ministry and how new members can get involved.
- Create the brochures, postcards, or flyers.
- Stock the connection center with new materials.
- Stock the mugging or first-time visitor gift area with new materials.

Step 4. Plan Phone Campaigns

Whether you are planting a church or reviving an existing congregation, phone campaigns can bring awareness to your church and also encourage people to come who might have been thinking about finding a church. In order to be most effective in your effort, purchase a crisscross directory of your community. The crisscross directory is sorted by street, so you will know you are speaking to people right there in your area. Determine a radius of people you want to reach, and order the crisscross directory accordingly. Once you have your phone numbers, set up a phone bank and organize a team of callers. Adapt the scripts in this guide to meet your needs. Train and prepare your callers to be warm, inviting, and positive at all times. Print the follow-up form in this guide as well, so that callers can note who requested further information.

Tasks:

- Determine the radius of your phone campaign.
- Buy a crisscross directory.
- Set up a phone bank.
- Organize and train callers.
- Print scripts for as many phone numbers as you call, so callers can write the information onto each script and store for follow up.
- After the phone campaign, gather scripts from callers and sort in order of desire for follow up.
- Follow up with callers who wanted more information about the church. Send them packets of information as well as a personal invitation to worship.
- Record in the church database for future mailings all addresses of callers who wanted more information.

Reproducibles (see Catch: Program Guide with DVD ROM)

- Phone Script
- Ring No Answer Script

Step 5. Prepare Newspaper and Radio Ads

Newspaper and radio spots can be incredible opportunities for making people aware of your church and its ministries. However, they can also be expensive. So you will want to be strategic about getting the most advertising for the least cost.

An ad in the faith section of your local newspaper is generally targeted for Christians who might have just moved to town and are looking for a church home. This is a perfectly noble advertising effort. However, if you want to communicate to non-religious or nominally religious Christians, you will have to advertise outside the faith section. Fortunately, listings in the community calendar are usually provided free or at minimal cost. What ministries, programs, or events might you put in the community calendar? Make sure your wording about the event or program is welcoming and inviting to people who have never been to your church or may never even have heard of it.

Another way to get newspaper coverage without the expense of an advertisement is to be in touch with the religion or community editor. When you have events that are newsworthy, be sure to check in with these editors to see if they would like to cover it. For instance, are your youth raising money for a mission project? Do you have an all-community event such as a churchwide yard sale, concert, race, or gathering? Get these events covered in the newspaper as a way to bring awareness to your church and its ministries.

Radio spots can be even more expensive than newspaper ads because of the recording costs. If you have the technology and funds, maximize your reach by advertising on a secular radio station instead of the local Christian station. Time your spot to promote a Christmas worship service, since many non-churchgoers make a point to attend a Christmas service. See the sample from Adam Hamilton included in this guide.

Most radio stations broadcast a community calendar or post one on their Web site. Make a point to list your events and community ministries on the community calendars of as many radio stations as possible—secular, Christian, even news stations.

Tasks

- Research the costs of advertising in the local newspaper, free newspapers, and radio stations.
- Decide if you have the funds and the technology to create excellent ads.
- If you decide to place an ad, have a professional designer and copywriter help you create the ad or a professional producer help with a radio spot.
- Make a list of all of the events, programs, or ministries that are appropriate for the community calendar.
- Assign a team member to research community calendars and to post events.
- Determine what ministries or events might be newsworthy, and assign someone to be in touch with the religion or community editor at the newspaper.

Reproducibles (see Catch: Program Guide with DVD ROM)

- Sample Radio Ad

Step 6. Equip Members to Invite Visitors

The best way to attract new people is to have members who are excited and then equip them to invite visitors to church. Evaluate how often you see your members bringing visitors. What can you do to communicate the importance of invitation and then equip your members to invite people? Consider making pocket New Testaments available to your members to carry in hopes that they may have an opportunity to give one away with a personal invitation to church.

In addition, create business cards with the church's name, address, Web site, and worship times, and make them readily available for members to hand out. You might even ask each member family to purchase one box of business cards so they always have some and are always thinking about inviting visitors.

Tasks

- Secure a stock of pocket New Testaments for members to give away to potential visitors.
- Create business cards with the church's name, address, Web site, and worship times that members can easily hand out with their personal invitation to church.

PHONE SCRIPT

Remember to smile! It comes across on the phone.

Show excitement and high energy!

Be a "caring caller." Listen for opportunities to connect and build relationships.

Make notes and fill in blanks.

Pray before you make each call.

Speak clearly.

> Hello, my name is _____ and I'm a volunteer with _____. How are you today / tonight? (Be prepared for someone *not* doing well. Be concerned and listen to their story, then offer consolation and pray for them if appropriate.)

No answer? Leave a message. See "Ring No Answer Script."

> We're making calls to let you know about something happening in our community. We want to invite you personally to our Easter / Christmas worship service.
> [or]
> We're preparing to launch a new church / ministry to serve our city. Do you already have a church home?
> [If yes] Then I want you to know what a joy it is to serve alongside you here in our city to reach people for Christ.
> [If no] Then I want you to know that I'm a part of an exciting church, and we're calling to invite people in the area to join us for _____.   The event is at [time] at [location]. We're a church committed to meeting the needs of our community, and building fellowship and connection with one another. Our worship services are inspiring, and we offer great programs for people of all ages. If you've been looking for a church where you can ask questions about faith in a safe environment, where you can find meaningful opportunities to serve in the community, and where you can feel at home, we hope you will check us out.
> May I send you some information? [If yes, get the mailing address.] [If no:] Okay, thank you for your time. We're excited to be part of the community. You can also check us out at _____.org.
> Thank you for your time, and have a great day / night. God Bless!

RING NO ANSWER SCRIPT
(LEAVE MESSAGE)

Hello, my name is _____ and I'm a volunteer with _____.
We're making calls to spread the word about our church. If you don't already have a church home,
we'd like to invite you to check us out at _____.org, or you can call us at _____.

If you've been looking for a church where you can ask questions about faith in a safe environment,
where you can find meaningful opportunities to serve the community, and where you can feel at
home, we hope that you'll check us out. We're meeting at [time] at [location]. Thank you and God
Bless!

SAMPLE RADIO AD

Here is a script from one of the radio ads that ran during the Christmas season:

The Gift on Behalf of Others

Are you looking for some last-minute gift ideas? Can't decide what to give someone who has everything?

Hi, I'm Adam Hamilton, senior pastor of the Church of the Resurrection. A friend recently gave me a great Christmas gift—a share of a sheep that was donated to a family in a third-world country. I recently gave a gift to a friend of ten meals provided in his honor to those who are homeless in a shelter here in Kansas City. If you're looking for a great gift to give someone who has everything, consider giving a gift in their honor to someone who has nothing. A gift of $10, $20, or $50 to area agencies that work with low-income people can make a difference and be a great way to let your friends and family know that you care about them and you care about others.

If you'd like help finding a way to give this kind of gift, check out our Web site at www.cor.org, where you can find links to area agencies and suggestions and opportunities for working directly with them to give gifts that really will make a difference. And if you don't yet have plans to attend a Christmas Eve candlelight service, I'd like to invite you to join us for one hour—an hour that will help you remember what Christmas is really all about.

2.
Making Visitors
Feel Welcome

2.
Making Visitors
Feel Welcome

Imagine being invited to a dinner party, but when you arrive at the house there is no place to park. All the parking spots closest to the house are already filled by the hosts and their immediate family members. Looking for a place to park your car, you circle the block several times. You finally park and make the long walk to the house, but when you get to the front door there is no one to greet you. The door is ajar. As you look inside you see people gathered, talking and laughing with one another, so hesitantly you walk in. The host appears to notice you have entered and nods politely but continues in a conversation with the others in the room.

When it comes time for the meal, there is no place for you at the table. The host of the party and other members of the immediate family have taken the best seats at the table. No one gets up to offer you a seat. As the meal is served, there are several unfamiliar dishes. No explanation is given about what they are or how they should be eaten. While standing in the corner, you watch others enjoy their meal while you are left feeling like an outsider, wondering why you were invited in the first place. You exit as quickly as possible.

Can you imagine a dinner party like this? The idea seems absurd, but in reality this scene is lived out every weekend in churches across the country. Invited guests (visitors) arrive but are not greeted at the door. When visitors come inside they see the hosts (church members) engaged in friendly conversations among themselves. When it comes time for the meal (worship), the best seats are taken, leaving visitors on the fringes. Worship practices are sometimes unfamiliar, and visitors may not be able to participate because they don't understand what is happening, or they don't know the words to songs and prayers that everyone else seems to have memorized. And then there is parking. Because most visitors arrive late, the parking spaces closest to the building are full and they are forced to park in the spaces farthest from the front door.

Many churches are blind to the fact that they are not practicing hospitality. Maybe it is because we confuse being friendly with being hospitable. Most churches are friendly, but usually with those who are already members. Hospitality, in contrast, should be focused specifically on receiving and treating guests and strangers in a warm and generous way.

Hospitality is part of our mission in the world. Churches should set the standard of what it means to be hospitable and welcoming, but too often we miss the mark. Nelson Searcy and Jennifer Dykes Henson write in their book *Fusion* (Regal Books, 2007),

> Unfortunately, we live in a culture in which the business world understands more about true expressions of hospitality than the Church does. . . . While hotels, restaurants and stores all around us serve their guests with intentional care, we often let ours wander in and out of our weekly services with no specific plan for showing them how important they are to us. (p. 42)

What is your plan for transforming your environment into one of welcome? Your initial interactions with visitors will help determine their willingness to connect. Their first impressions of your church are important and may be the deciding factor as to whether they return.

Their experience begins in the parking lot—before they even enter the building. Does your building communicate that this is a place that honors God? Is the building well maintained? Is the landscaping manicured? Is trash contained and hidden? Is directional signage visible? Is parking accessible and easy to find? The truth is that if visitors experience chaos in the parking lot or can't find a place to park, it is unlikely they will even enter the building.

Visitors want to be welcomed. In fact, they expect to be welcomed, but they don't want to be overwhelmed. Visitors are looking for a welcome that feels authentic, so it is important to train volunteers to be gracious and warm but not overbearing. Greeters should be clearly identified. Because the greeter is the first point of contact inside the building, the interaction between the arriving guest and the greeter in many ways sets the tone for worship. Greeters should always lead visitors where they want to go, not just point them in the right direction.

Excellent signage helps your visitors feel at ease. This includes signage marking the location of restrooms, the sanctuary, children's areas, and a general information area. Signage outside the building should not be overlooked, as it provides the first point of reference for your guests as they arrive.

Signage helps self-direct visitors to their desired location, but there are times when visitors would prefer a personal touch. Having your leaders wear nametags gives a visual signal as to whom they should ask. We encourage staff, church leaders, and members to wear nametags at all times.

Another way to make visitors feel at home and let them know you are expecting them is to provide coffee and refreshments. Refreshments help form a positive first impression and foster an environment that encourages people to linger and talk as they drink their coffee. Fostering a visitor-friendly environment is important in your lobby area, but it continues into the sanctuary. Ushers not only provide assistance in helping worship run smoothly; they also serve as the initial greeting for guests into the sanctuary as they assist visitors to open seats.

Making your church outwardly focused means you have made it a priority to have seats available for visitors. In the story of the paralyzed man brought to Jesus on a stretcher, the place where Jesus taught was so crowded with religious leaders—those on the "inside"—that those on the outside were not able to get close. Similarly, in churches we often don't have seats available because all the members have crowded in. Of course, in this story the man's friends were creative and lowered him through the roof. Let's not make it that hard on our visitors! Your church leaders must make it a priority to have open seats available for visitors.

Have you ever been in a church where you've been told not to sit in a particular seat or pew because it is "so and so's place"? Yes, this even happens from time to time at our church. Several years ago, our senior pastor's mother arrived for worship. A few moments after finding a seat, she felt a gentle tap on her shoulder. As she turned, she was greeted by someone who politely but insistently asked her to move because she was sitting in their seat. Our pastor's mother moved, but you have probably already guessed the rest of the story. The following week's sermon included a few pointers about seating.

Once visitors are seated, helping them feel a part of the worship service is also important. During worship, these small tips will help a visitor feel more a part of the experience:

- All the people who speak in the service should introduce themselves. This eliminates the perception by visitors that they aren't part of the group because they don't know everyone's name.
- Include a time of greeting at the beginning of the service, but try to design this time in such a way that visitors will feel comfortable and not stand out.
- Explain each transition in the worship service.
- Print the words to songs, prayers, and liturgy in the bulletin or on video screens.
- Get information from visitors by passing an attendance notebook, so you can follow up with them.

- Include information in your bulletin for first-time visitors, such as how to get additional information after worship, where to go if you are a nursing mother, whom to ask for help if you have special needs or require first aid or emergency assistance, and how to purchase or check out a DVD or CD of the sermon.
- After worship, provide a well-marked location where guests can ask questions, get additional information, or register for classes and events. The volunteers at this location should be among your most highly trained hospitality team members. Our location is called the Connection Point and is central to all that is happening in our lobby area.

People matter to God. The principles of providing customer service and a welcoming environment should be consistent in all ministries and programs of the church, not just in worship. By transforming your church into a welcoming environment, you will create space for visitors to experience the love of God. This may mean that visitors will take their coffee into your sanctuary, ask to register for a class after the deadline, or pick up their children from Sunday school ten minutes late. Having rules and standards is important, but also keep your purpose and mission of welcoming visitors in mind as you address these situations with your guests. Now is the time to plan so visitors will know how important they are to you as you practice hospitality.

Work the Steps

Step 1. Evaluate Signage

Imagine a minivan pulling into your parking lot for the first time. Inside is a mom and dad, a middle-schooler, a second-grader, and a one-year-old. They are arriving about five minutes late. Where will they have to park? Do they know which door to enter? Once they are inside, do they know where to take each of their children? They need to make a stop at the restroom first; will they find the closest one to them?

Take your team around the building—including the parking lot—and look at your facility through the eyes of this family. Make a list of necessary changes and work with the trustees to implement them.

Tasks:

- Evaluate the presence, helpfulness, and quality of outdoor signage. Post signs for the following at every parking lot entrance:

The location of the sanctuary
Parking for those with disabilities
Designated parking for first-time visitors
Visitor entrance
Location of special events

- Evaluate the presence, helpfulness, and quality of indoor signage. Designate and install room numbers for all meeting rooms. At every major hub and important fork, post signs for the following locations in the church building:

Sanctuary
Restrooms
Nursery
Children's ministry
Youth room

Step 2. Invite and Train Volunteer Parking Lot Greeters

When you have designated parking spots for visitors, assign some volunteers to greet them right there in the parking lot and help them get where they need to go. Don't smother or overwhelm them; simply welcoming and directing them to the right entrance can make visitors feel more relaxed and at home.

Tasks:

- Determine whether your flow of traffic requires a crew of people to direct traffic before and after the service. If you need this ministry, invite some volunteers and begin helping visitors and members experience your hospitality before they ever get inside.
- Determine how many parking lot attendants you will need. Do you have a large campus with several entrances and exits? Do you have visitor parking spots near multiple entrances? How can you most effectively greet and assist visitors without overwhelming them?

Step 3. Invite and Train a Volunteer Team of Greeters

Remember that dinner party we imagined at the beginning of this chapter? Recall how it felt when you were not greeted at the door but rather had to make your way in and fend for yourself. You don't want your visitors apprehensively stepping in the door and wondering what to do next. You want a team of people whose job it is to joyfully greet, welcome, and help visitors get where they want to be. This is such an important ministry and can have such an impact on your welcoming efforts.

Recruit and train a team of volunteers to carry out this ministry. Communicate to them that they should refrain from lengthy conversations with current members while they are serving. You don't want a greeter to get caught up in a conversation with a friend while a visitor walks through the door, sees people chatting, and doesn't know where to go. Greeters should be visible, wear nametags, and be willing to walk visitors to their destination instead of just pointing and giving directions.

Tasks:

- Announce a greeter signup and training.
- Recruit and train greeters.
- Give each volunteer a copy of the Greeter Ministry handout (see Appendix and DVD ROM).
- Begin greeting ministry immediately.

Step 4. Encourage Members to Wear Nametags

You know that feeling when you meet a person for the first time and not even five minutes later you can't remember their name? Or maybe you've been on the other end of the conversation and have, only moments before, introduced yourself, then realized someone clearly can't remember your name when they try to introduce you to someone else. To remove this barrier and make everyone feel at home, encourage your congregation and staff to wear nametags at all gatherings. This small thing can make a huge difference in making your church a welcoming congregation.

Tasks:

- Determine the budget and start-up arrangements for wearing nametags. Will you use disposable stick-ons or plastic clip-ons? Where will you store reusable nametags so they are convenient to grab and go? How will you invite visitors to create and wear a nametag as they arrive?
- Buy supplies, set up a nametag station, and get started.

Step 5. Keep it Clean

Visitors don't appreciate a musty, dingy church building where old bulletins are strewn about, weeds are sprouting through cracks in the parking lot, and dying flowers fill the window sills. Of course this is an exaggeration, but you get the point. Encourage your ministry teams, staff, and congregants to work together in keeping the facility up and looking its best—inside and out.

Tasks:

- Meet with the trustees or building committee to determine what needs to be done to clean up or fix up around the facility. Do you need to paint the children's hall? Do the toys in the nursery need cleaning? Does the flowerbed around the church sign need weeding?
- Assess the entire facility and work together to beautify the space and make it more inviting for visitors. Make a list, and appoint people to handle each item.

Step 6. Create a Visitor-Friendly Worship Service

The worship service is one of the most important ways to show hospitality. Think about your worship service. Can visitors catch on easily, or will they feel as if they may as well be on the planet Mars? We don't need to sacrifice our identity to make visitors feel welcomed, but we do need to explain things along the way so that inexperienced churchgoers don't become stressed out by wondering what to do next.

Tasks:

- Meet with the pastor and worship planning team to discuss goals for welcoming and explaining worship transitions.
- Write sample scripts for the following transitions: welcome to worship, invitation to greet one another, invitation to fill out attendance notebooks.
- Talk with the pastor and the worship-planning team about how to explain each transition smoothly and effectively—standing, sitting, singing, praying—in order to help visitors anticipate what's coming next.
- Talk with the pastor and worship-planning team about making sure words to songs, prayers, and readings are projected on the screen or written in the bulletin—even the Lord's Prayer and the Doxology.

Reproducibles (see Catch: Program Guide with DVD ROM*)*

- Welcoming Language for Worship

Step 7. Establish a Connection Point

It is so important to have a central location that visitors can see and access easily, where they can get answers to questions, sign up for programs, and make any necessary connections. Think of this area as your Connection Point. Display current program brochures, first-time visitor packets, and any other helpful materials. Set up a computer with Internet access so volunteers can register visitors for classes or send e-mails to program ministry leaders with questions or requests.

Tasks:

- Identify where you will place the Connection Point
- Determine what the Connection Point will look like. Will you use tables, order a custom counter, purchase a moveable display?
- Hang a sign in a visible place. Whether the sign is a banner or just letters on the wall, make sure that when you walk through the door, you can see a path leading to the Connection Point.
- Recruit and train a volunteer team to serve in the Connection Point. Team members should be outgoing, friendly, do-what-it-takes kind of people. Give each volunteer a copy of the Connection Point Ministry handout (see Appendix and DVD ROM).
- Develop a first-time visitor packet. Determine what should be included in the packet.
- Secure materials from all program ministries for visitor packets.
- Meet with staff about signups for current classes and any information they would want volunteers to share with visitors.
- Determine a system to provide weekly updated information about the ministries of the church to the volunteers who serve at the center.
- Develop a system for follow up should a volunteer not be able to provide the answer to a specific question or request.

Step 8. Establish or Improve Coffee Time

Providing coffee and snacks creates a coffee-shop feel that encourages people to linger in conversation and feel like part of the group. Set up coffee and refreshment stations before and after worship. If possible, arrange coffee tables, couches, or comfortable chairs to foster conversations and community.

Tasks:

- Determine the location of your coffee station.
- Recruit volunteers to set up, serve, and clean up.
- Determine how to create a coffee-shop feel within the parameters of your space.
- Purchase furniture and supplies as needed.
- Begin coffee time as soon as possible.

Step 9. Make Room

Even when your sanctuary is nearly full, there is usually one place that is available for latecomers. Can you think of where that is? You guessed it—the front row. If you are visiting a church for the first time and walk into a crowded sanctuary a few minutes late, how do you feel if you have to take that long walk to the first row? Not very good, right? It is so important to communicate to your congregation that one of the best ways they can serve visitors is just by scooting up a row or two. Encourage members to sit in the front rows and leave the back rows open for late-arriving visitors to sneak in without being conspicuous.

The same applies to the parking lot. Encourage members who are able to park in the most distant spaces to do so, and leave the closer spots for others. We tend to seek out the very best parking spot and grab it if we can. Help your members view taking a distant parking space on Sunday morning as an act of service and ministry.

Tasks:

- Encourage members to welcome visitors by sitting in the front rows and parking in the most distant spaces. Remind the congregation that elderly people, those with disabilities, and families with small children should feel free to sit or park wherever is most convenient.
- Train ushers to seat members from the front rows to the back, so there are always seats in the back rows for late-arriving visitors.

Step 10. Care for Children

Gone are the days when you walked into a church building and had an assumption of safety for your child, or when you could just drop off your child in the nursery without a pager, cell phone, or check-in procedure. Today's parents expect a system for check-in and check-out, notification when a parent is needed, and a bright, fun, clean space for kids. When you focus on creating a welcoming environment that's committed to hospitality, be sure to create a children's ministry where parents feel their children will be safe and loved.

Children's safety should be the highest priority. No matter the size of your church, a well-organized system for check-in and check-out is essential. Design a procedure in which children can only be released back to a parent or designated caregiver. You can use a computerized bar scan system, matching nametags, a number system with stickers, or any number of other ways to match parents and children. Having a simple and effective system for check-in and check-out will ease the fears of visitors and provide the best hospitality.

Besides paying attention to safety, be intentional about creating an engaging environment for children, using bright colors, age-appropriate toys and activities, and interactive experiences. The goal is for children to enter the space and say, "Wow!" the way they do when arriving at their favorite pizza place or theme park. Creating a "Wow!" space does not have to be expensive. Enlist creative volunteers who will be excited about using their gifts and talents to improve your space. You will be surprised at the difference made by doing something as simple as changing the paint color from "church taupe" to a brighter and more vivid one.

Tasks:

- Evaluate the current safety procedures for children, including a system for check-in and check-out.
- Identify what is needed to make the current procedure smoother and more efficient, or create a new system to improve safety.
- Recruit and train high-energy and loving volunteers that can help parents find the check-in station, guide children to classrooms, and feel that they can walk away knowing that their kids are safe and ready for a great experience.
- Evaluate the appearance of the children's area. Does it look like a place that would get kids excited? How can you create a "Wow!" experience for your children?
- Design an improved children's ministry area, and execute the plan as soon as possible.

Step 11. Evaluate Phone Greeting and Voice Mail Information

Your church telephone is often the front line of visitor connection. Do you have a receptionist, paid or volunteer, who warmly greets callers and directs their calls? What happens when no one is there to answer? Does your voice mail message give information that would be helpful to potential visitors, such as your location and worship times?

When we are intentional about transforming every aspect of our church into a welcoming and hospitable environment, even something as basic as voice mail becomes important.

Tasks:

- Evaluate current phone greeting and voice mail messages.
- Make any necessary changes to ensure that the greeting script is consistent, warm, and helpful.
- Make any necessary changes to the voice mail message to ensure that callers can get directions and worship times.

Reproducibles (see Catch: Program Guide with DVD ROM):

- First-Time Visitor Touch Points

WELCOMING LANGUAGE FOR WORSHIP

Greeting Script

Welcome to [church name]! We are so excited that you're here today! My name is [speaker's name]. I am [speaker's role or position], and we are so grateful that you've chosen to worship with us today!

Let's take a moment to welcome those sitting around you. Will you turn and say hello to a few people sitting around you?

We've gathered here to worship God, to sing praise to God's name, to lift up our prayers for thanksgiving and confession. We've come to lay before God our concerns. It's our hope that God will speak to you through the special music and the readings of Scripture and the message, that you might know God's will for your life. We hope you will leave renewed, refreshed, and ready to serve God in the world.

With that in mind, let's take a moment to pray.

Invitation to Fill Out Attendance Notebooks

The ushers are passing out the attendance notebooks. If you would take a few moments to let us know you were here, we would be most appreciative. If you're a first-time visitor, please notice the information provided for you. If you're a guest or a part of this congregation, please fill out the prayer cards to let us know how we can pray with and for you this week. As the notebooks get to the end of the row, please pass them back down the row, and look to see who is sitting near you so you can welcome those in your row by name at the end of our worship service.

As the notebook make their way down the rows, I want to take a minute to let you know what's going on in our community this week. [Make announcements.]

FIRST-TIME VISITOR TOUCH POINTS

Below are the "touch points" or contacts that a first-time visitor has available and may have received prior to, on the day of, and following their first visit to the church.

TOUCHES PRIOR TO WORSHIP SERVICE

- Web site, social media, or newspaper ad with worship times, phone number, and address.
- Contact with a receptionist during the week or Sunday mornings with voice mail backup that gives worship times, styles of worship, and directions to the church.
- Mailer received in home or given to a visitor by another member.
- Contact in the community through a service project or community outreach event, or by an outside group using the church building for an event.
- Volunteer prep teams prepare seatbacks, notebooks, bulletins, and coffee mugs during the week for weekend services.
- The worship team decorates the sanctuary and chapel beautifully for holidays.

TOUCHES ON THE DAY OF FIRST-TIME VISIT TO WORSHIP SERVICE

Before service

- Permanent signage is in place for first-time visitor parking, with instructions for visitors to turn on hazard lights as a signal to the parking attendants.
- Parking attendants on duty to direct traffic.
- Greeters located at all building entrances to give a warm welcome to visitors as they enter our church. Greeters wear a bright "greeter" button so they are easily identified.
- Guides will help visitors feel comfortable in our facilities by showing them the way to important locations, such as sanctuary, childcare, classrooms, and restrooms.
- Volunteers at the Connection Point (information center) are available to answer ministry questions or escort visitors to classes.
- Volunteers serve coffee before and after worship services.
- Ushers on duty at the sanctuary doors hand out bulletins and welcome everyone.
- Ushers on duty inside the sanctuary handle visitor seating, or ask for number in group and signal another usher to invite them to a seating area.

During service

- Acolytes carry in the cross and light the altar candles to remind us of Christ's presence with us.
- Service of worship planned with a first-time visitor in mind, engaging the congregation to encounter God through song, prayer, Scripture, and sermon.
- Time of greeting prior to the start of worship.
- Ushers pass attendance notebooks when directed to do so from the pulpit. (It is helpful that someone with authority asks everyone to sign in and that visitors see others signing in.)
- On days we serve communion, the communion team serves Holy Communion.

After service

- Ushers remove attendance sheets from notebooks and place them in two stacks—one for visitors and one for members.
- Volunteer teams record attendance in the database.

- First-time visitor attendance sheets are pulled from the visitor stack and given to the mapping team. These volunteers use the Internet to generate maps to first-time visitors' homes.
- Mappers place the maps in coffee mugs that are stuffed with a church brochure and other information. Mappers then place the mugs on shelves, according to zip code.
- Mug delivery team volunteers (a.k.a. "muggers") pick up the mugs and deliver them to first-time visitors' homes. Our goal is to deliver mugs within 48 hours of the first visit.
- First-time visitor information is entered into the database.

TOUCHES FOLLOWING FIRST-TIME VISIT

- First-time visitor letters are prepared on Monday evenings following completion of all data entry. The letter welcomes and thanks the visitor for worshiping with us. Letters are mailed on Tuesday.
- After visitor has attended three or more times within a three-month period, they receive a phone call, letter, or email with an invitation to Coffee with the Pastors.
- Weekday hospitality team volunteers are available at information booths to assist anyone with questions or directions to classrooms.
- Guided tours of the church are offered on weekends. Tours may also be scheduled by request.

3.
Connecting and Following Up
With Visitors

3.
Connecting and Following Up With Visitors

I was raised in a United Methodist church, was active in the youth group, and then went to college and became (what I now know is) a nominal Christian. I attended church each Easter Sunday and on Christmas Eve, and I was married in a church, but I was not growing spiritually or practicing my faith.

After the birth of our children, my husband and I knew that we wanted to find a church. We wanted our children to grow up in the church, but we were also looking for relationships with other young parents who were going through some of the same life situations that we were experiencing. After looking in the Yellow Pages for the United Methodist church closest to where we lived, we made our first visit. The preacher was a great communicator, the music was excellent, and people seemed friendly. After our first visit, we were excited and hoped to connect with others. From the bulletin we learned about a sand volleyball team for young couples. This sounded like a good way to connect with other people close to our age, so we completed the sign-up form, turned it in as instructed, and waited. No one called for a week; no one called for two weeks; still, after a month, no one called. Taking the initiative, I called the church office and left a message. Again, no one from the church called. Next, we tried signing up to play on the co-ed softball team, but no one called for a week; then two weeks passed without a call. We even inquired about Sunday school classes geared for young adults, but each of our attempts to get involved in the church failed. Not surprisingly, after a few months of unsuccessful attempts to connect and form relationships, our worship attendance decreased. During all of this, no one at the church noticed our desire to connect on a deeper level.

A year or so after our failed attempts to get involved in church, we began hearing about a new church that met in a funeral home. My husband suggested we visit, despite my noting that the location was not convenient to our house. When we arrived, there was a young man on the sidewalk greeting people as they came in for worship. As we approached, he introduced himself, asked our names, and told us he was glad we had come to worship. Once inside, I discovered the sidewalk greeter was the senior pastor.

During the worship service, an attendance notebook was passed, and each person was asked to sign in. Later that afternoon, there was a knock on the door. I answered and was surprised to see the senior pastor of the church we had visited a few hours before, standing on my doorstep. I thought to myself, "I wonder what he wants? I hope he doesn't want to come in and visit." I opened the door and he quickly said, "I don't want to come in, but I just wanted you to know how much we enjoyed having you in worship this morning. We hope you'll come back. As a token of our appreciation, I've brought you a coffee mug." He asked if we had any questions and, remembering we had toddlers, invited us to an Easter egg hunt the church was hosting the following Saturday.

On Saturday, I decided to give the Easter egg hunt a try. I took both my children and, in all honesty, drove to the event feeling some reservations. I was very nervous about going because I did not know anyone. When I arrived, I was greeted by a friendly volunteer who directed my children and me to a circle where three other families were decorating Easter baskets in preparation for the hunt that was to follow. While in our circles, we were given the opportunity to visit and connect with each other in a well-planned, organized, and comfortable way. I left feeling that I had actually made some connections with other young families, and my kids had tons of fun.

The following week, I signed up at the church and volunteered to serve during Vacation Bible School. I received a return telephone call the next day. I was amazed at how quickly we were getting connected. In the first year of attending that church, we played on a co-ed softball team, volunteered for committee work, served on several mission projects, and joined the church, becoming active members.

Now I serve on the staff of that church, and I am committed to reaching out to other non-religious and nominally religious people, as my husband and I were when we began this journey. I am thankful that the church was so committed to its vision that we were "caught." And many of the families I connected with at that first Easter egg hunt have become some of our closest friends and companions in Christ.

The difference between our experiences at the two churches was the degree of follow up. It may seem obvious, but if you want to integrate new people into the life of your church, you must be intentional about follow up. Excellent hospitality determines whether or not a visitor will further engage in the life of the church.

Some churches that provide excellent hospitality don't always follow up, perhaps because it is time-consuming and requires effort on the part of your leadership and volunteer teams. As you may discover, so much of what you do to "catch" visitors overlaps with your marketing, hospitality, and follow-up and connection efforts. Through direct-mail pieces and personal invitations, you may attract several first-time visitors weekly. As visitors arrive, they are focused first on getting their children to the nurseries, locating the sanctuary, finding a seat, and orienting themselves with the surroundings. The hospitality ministry involves greeters, ushers, and building location signs that help a visitor get acclimated. Once inside the sanctuary, your visitor-friendly worship service puts newcomers at ease, because they are not identified as "outsiders."

Although first-time visitors do not want to be singled out, most want to feel they can be a part of something. Effective follow-up strategies will help visitors discover ways they can quickly connect and will help your church begin to build relationships with non-Christian and nominally Christian people in your community.

Follow up begins with knowing who are your visitors. Decide on an efficient way to collect information about visitors. One way is to pass an attendance notebook during each worship service. Because newcomers do not want to be singled out, ask everyone to "sign in and let us know you are here." Consider these three reasons for taking attendance:

1. It shows the congregation that you value relationships and connection. After you request that each person sign in, you can also announce to the congregation, "After each person in your row has signed in, pass the attendance notebook back down the row. Look to see who is sitting next to you, and greet that person by name at the conclusion of our worship service."

2. It provides contact information so you can effectively follow up with visitors. It also records attendance information of your members so you can quickly follow up if a member has been missing from weekly worship. At our church, if members miss, one of our connection team members makes a personal phone call to check on them.

3. Having a good database provides access to information so you can communicate more effectively with your congregation. There are many software products designed specifically to help churches facilitate this type of follow up.

Another method of collecting information is to use a communication card. This card asks for visitors' contact information and possibly feedback on their experience. Some churches insert these cards into the bulletins, make them available in the chair-back pocket, or invite visitors to an information desk at the conclusion of the service. A communication card is a great tool for collecting both contact information and initial feedback about a visitor's experience. However, the challenge is getting the cards turned in. Some churches invite visitors to their information desk for a complimentary gift as an incentive.

Remember, while collecting data is an important part of your follow-up strategy, it is not the entire strategy. Your follow-up strategy needs to include a good way to invite the visitor to engage in the life of your church. At Church of the Resurrection, we deliver coffee mugs with information about the church to every first-time visitor. We use the contact information received on the attendance notebook and online mapping tools to print the directions to each visitor's home. Coffee mugs are organized by zip code, and volunteer "muggers" pick up the mugs in their zip code and personally deliver them to the homes of the visitors. Our goal is for each visitor to be "mugged" within forty-eight hours of his or her first visit to our church.

Some churches bake bread or other bakery items and, immediately following a worship service, deliver them to the homes of their visitors. Other churches host receptions where visitors grab a cup of coffee and hear information about the church and how they can be involved. There are many ways to let your visitors know their visit is important. Discover what works best for your church, and then do it. Follow up requires time. Make it a high priority and stay committed.

In addition to providing a mug, we mail each first-time visitor a letter from our senior pastor, reiterating his thanks for their visit. The letter provides contact information so visitors have direct access to someone, should they have questions. After the third visit, we mail another follow-up letter. This letter is more specific about getting connected into the life of the church and begins to suggest the importance of being in a small group.

This same level of high-priority follow up should be consistent throughout all ministry areas, not just in worship. Visitors to any of our program ministries receive an e-mail or phone call from the leader, letting them know we are glad they visited and hope they will return. You will retain visitors most effectively if they can quickly find a place to get connected at your church and if someone calls them by name with an invitation to come back. Churches that are effective at retaining visitors offer quick opportunities for visitors to get involved.

Effective follow up and connection requires a team of committed people. Find volunteers in your church who are excellent at customer service and detail. These are the people who will make sure that nothing and no one falls through the cracks. However, follow up is not the responsibility of just that team; it is the job of everyone in your church. Returning e-mails, following up voice mails, and responding in a timely fashion to questions are values that everyone in your church must hold.

God cares about your visitors. As you share the good news of the gospel, the commitment you make to follow up demonstrates that you care about them, too.

> Because we loved you so much, we were delighted to share with you not
> only the gospel of God but our lives as well. (1 Thessalonians 2:8 NIV)

Work the Steps

Step 1. Collect Information

Evaluate your current data management system. Do you have attendance pads or connection cards in place? How efficient and effective is your data entry and follow-up procedure? Do you need to stop what you're currently doing and take another approach? Change the culture of your church from anonymity to "it matters to us that you are here."

Tasks:

- Determine your attendance strategy.
- Design the attendance sheet or communication card.
- Order attendance notebooks or communication cards.
- Determine the software or system you will use to input the attendance data.
- Develop a data entry ministry. Create a volunteer job description; invite and train team members.
- Designate an area in the church where the team will input the data.
- Create a system of printing out first-time visitor information and maps for "mugging" or gift delivery.

Step 2. Begin a Mugging Ministry

At our church, the reason we give mugs to first-time visitors is because a mug is an everyday item that can remind people about our church and their experience with us. We print our logo on the mugs and fill them with information about our church and ministries. Some churches take bread or other items. While bread is a beautiful symbol of hospitality and welcome, once the bread is eaten there isn't that everyday item going in and out of the cupboard, reminding visitors about their experience with the church. Think through what item you want to give. If you decide on mugs, place a large order to lower costs, and ask your members to support the ministry by purchasing a mug for their home or office.

Tasks

- Determine what your first-time visitor gift will be.
- Allow time for any necessary design work.
- Get bids on mugs or other items and choose the best bid.
- Work with connection center volunteers to get current information about church ministries and programs with which to fill mugs.
- Prepare a first-time visitor letter.
- Prepare a script for the delivery team to use.
- Designate an area where your delivery team will pick up the mugs or other gifts and assignments.
- Determine the timeframe in which the visit should be made.
- Recruit and train volunteers for a first-time visitor gift delivery ministry. Give each volunteer a copy of the Mugging Ministry handout (see Appendix and DVD ROM)
- Develop a follow-up process to verify that all first-time visitors have been "mugged" or gifted in some way.

Reproducibles (see Catch: Program Guide with DVD ROM)

- First-Time Visitor Letter

Step 3. Follow Up Again After Three Visits

A visitor attends your church for the first time and is greeted and made to feel welcome, then receives a gift, information, and a letter all in a matter of days after that first visit. Following the third visit, make sure to check in again and help that person or family engage more deeply in the church community. Depending on the size of your congregation, develop a strategy in which either the pastor, another staff member, or a team of volunteers makes personal, in-home visits with third-time visitors to answer questions, share stories, and pray together.

Tasks:

- Work with the pastors to determine if their schedules allow for in-home visits or if other staff or volunteers will be assigned this task.
- Develop a system of automatically identifying three-time visitors. Decide: Who will make this list? Can your data management software generate a list each Monday? Who is the point person to make the connection, and who will follow up?

- Send a letter from the pastor to all three-time visitors (see sample).
- Recruit and train a team of volunteers if needed to make in-home visits. These people should know and love the church well and feel comfortable sharing their faith and praying for the visitors.

Reproducibles (see Catch: Program Guide with DVD ROM)
- Third-Time Visitor Letter

Step 4. Be Diligent in all Connection and Follow-Up Strategies

When you cast the net wide and fish for people in your community, take every precaution to avoid having any visitors fall through the cracks. We want to catch people with the love and grace of God and help them deepen their discipleship. Always evaluate the connection points to make sure that you are making every effort to connect people to ministries and inviting them to make a home in your congregation.

Each ministry area should be intentional about finding ways that a new person can connect easily and quickly into that ministry. In adult discipleship we regularly launch new small groups, Bible studies, classes, and service projects so people never have long to wait before getting connected into one of them. Our children and student ministry areas also have easy, ongoing entry points for new children and youth to get connected. Assimilating into the life of the church as quickly as possible is key to retaining visitors.

Timely follow-up is a high value at our church. We ask all our staff and ministry leaders to return phone calls and e-mails within twenty-four hours. We are also careful to set out-of-office responses on voice mail and e-mail so that anyone who contacts us knows when a follow-up reply might be expected.

Tasks:

- Continue to review, update, and stock the Connection Point with current information.
- Communicate the need for connecting and following up to every programming and worship conversation until the system is in place and working smoothly.
- Make a point to review follow-up procedures regularly to ensure that they are effective and that connections are being made.

FIRST-TIME VISITOR LETTER

Dear _____,

Thank you for visiting [church name]. My hope is that you found the worship service uplifting and meaningful, and I want you to know that we would love to have you return again this coming weekend.

I also want you to know that we care about creating a great experience for our visitors. It is important to us and we welcome your feedback on how we did. Please take a moment to complete a very brief survey at [church Web site address]. As a small token of our appreciation, we have included with this letter a certificate for complimentary coffee. We hope you'll receive this with our thanks for helping us improve.

We've found that people connect into the life of our church quite easily. And making an early connection in service to others or through participation in a ministry of the church can make all the difference. If you or a friend or family member would like to hear about becoming more involved, please drop by the Connection Point at church or visit our Web site.

We hope that you will join us again for worship. And, if you are looking for a church home, we hope you'll get connected at [church name]. It would be an honor to be your church family.

Thank you again for your feedback. It is greatly appreciated.

Grace and Peace,

THIRD-TIME VISITOR LETTER

Dear _____,

We are so glad you are worshiping with us, and we pray that your experience has been a blessing. If you do not already have a church home, we hope you will consider being part of our congregation.

Though we are a growing church, most people find connecting into the life of our congregation easy. To explore ways to get connected, please stop by our Connection Point at church. We look forward to helping you connect with people who share your interests. Connecting with a "small group" makes it easier to feel at home here, and we offer a wide variety of small groups, classes, and activities to choose from. If you would like to learn more about the church on your own, please visit our Web site _____, which will answer questions you may have about our church.

If you think you might be interested in membership, I invite you to our next Coffee with the Pastors event on [date]. We will meet in [location]. Coffee with the Pastors provides additional information about the church and will help you discover how you can become connected. After the event, you can decide if you are ready to become a member of the church. To attend, simply let us know that you are coming by visiting [Web site address], or just call [person or office and phone number].

Again, we are very pleased that you joined us for worship! We would love to help you grow in your faith and share fellowship together. To speak with someone personally, please contact the church office at _____.

We have a passion for helping people connect into the life of the church!

In Christ,

4.
Inviting Others
to Grow in Faith

4.
Inviting Others
to Grow in Faith

Discipleship calls individuals to a higher level of commitment. In order to help individuals on that journey, you must begin with the end in mind. At our church, we have defined a deeply committed Christian as an individual who knows, loves, and serves God. Jesus' discipleship model was fairly simple. He called people to make a greater commitment, invited them to follow him, modeled the life for them, provided experiences for their growth, sent them out to practice, and then told them to go out and do likewise.

So how do we invite people to make a greater commitment and then guide them on their journey? First, we must be clear about where we are leading people. We must be clear about our purpose statement. It should guide everything you do. It should inspire and challenge. We also define a deeply committed Christian as someone who is becoming theologically informed, spiritually transformed, and who is serving Christ daily in the world. We shortened this definition and called it Our Journey: Knowing, Loving, and Serving God. We feel this best captures where we are leading people as we invite them to make a greater commitment on the journey. This definition helps our ministry leaders think more strategically about the ministries offered, the classes taught, and the events hosted. Do they lead people to the destination of knowing, loving, and serving God? If something doesn't accomplish this, we don't do that particular event or offer that particular class.

We also created an "easy to navigate" route for a new member who might be looking for direction as he or she takes a next step. We recognize there are multiple ways to get to the destination, but instead of overwhelming an individual with options, we offer a recommended path and provide printed directions. Recommending the best practical resources for spiritual growth is becoming one of the new roles church leaders can play on behalf of their members in light of the twenty-first-century information-overload age.

Churches do this differently. Some offer new believer classes that individuals take in a progression. Some offer membership classes. There are a number of ideas and methods to help individuals in their next steps. Our philosophy on membership is to set the threshold low for joining, but to have high expectations once someone becomes a member. We don't have prerequisite classes or expectations of people before they can become members of the church. After people have visited three times, they receive an invitation to Coffee with the Pastor—a fellowship event where individuals are invited to the church for an information gathering to meet the pastor(s) and hear more about the church. At the end of the event, they are given an invitation to consider membership.

Membership expectations include weekly worship participation, growing in faith apart from worship, serving inside and outside the walls of the church, and giving in proportion to one's income, with a tithe being the goal. We have found that the best way to help our members live into these expectations is to encourage them to be committed to a small group. Small groups are where individuals grow and live out their faith in the context of community on the journey to becoming deeply committed Christians.

Like most destinations, there are multiple ways to get connected to a small group. We have many options available through women's and men's ministries, teaching events, and service opportunities. Small groups are important to the life of the church. Bible study is a key focus of the group's experience, but encouragement, accountability, and care for group members is a vital component. In addition, small group members serve together in mission in the community and world, and they serve one another.

While we recognize that simply committing to be a member of a church and participating in a learning community and small group will not equal life transformation, it is our hope that this path provides momentum and movement toward it. In Hebrews 10:25, we read a reminder not to give up meeting together, as some are in the habit of doing, but to encourage one another. In what ways does your pathway encourage new members so they have a sense of what it means to be the church, a sense of belonging and connectedness so they will not want to give up meeting? What is important as you help people on the journey is to be clear about where you are taking them, have a plan to get them there, and provide clear, easy-to-navigate directions. What resources, or directions, are you providing to help individuals on the journey?

Work the Steps

Step One: Invite Returning Visitors to Join

After a visitor has been in worship three times, invite them to a membership class. Host a membership event and give it a name, such as Coffee with the Pastors. Send personal invitations to returning visitors inviting them to this event. Post a public invitation in the Sunday bulletin and the monthly or weekly newsletter. Provide childcare for the event and serve refreshments before or after. As guests arrive, hand out nametags and folders of information about the church and membership expectations as well as the membership form.

The purpose of Coffee with the Pastors is for the pastor to tell his or her story and vision for the church, and for program staff to talk about the various ministries in your church. In addition, take this opportunity to explain that while there is low expectation for visitors, there is a defined set of expectations of what it means to be a member. Explain that members are asked to be present in worship regularly and attend worship elsewhere when they are traveling. Members are asked to seek opportunities to grow in faith by joining a small group. Members are asked to give their time in service and mission. And members are asked to give proportionately to their income, working toward a tithe.

After a time of question and answer, invite those who wish to join to fill out the membership form (see sample). Encourage those who may not be ready to join to continue praying about it; follow up with them regularly to see where they are in making their decision. Celebrate your new members during the next worship service. Invite them to stand and take their membership vows. Welcome them and invite your congregation to greet them after the service.

Tasks:

- Work with the pastor to determine a regular schedule for Coffee with the Pastors events.
- Determine where they will be held.
- Create membership packets with information about the church and the membership form.
- Assign volunteers to host a refreshments and nametag station.
- Send out personal invitations from the pastor inviting returning members to the event.
- Work with the pastor and the program staff to plan the gathering and prepare the order of service.

- Collect any membership forms that are filled out and give to the appropriate data entry contact.
- Celebrate the new members at the next worship service and invite them to take their membership vows.
- Follow up with any visitors who were not ready to join the church and stay in touch with them regularly.
- One week after joining, send new members a Letter to New Members (see sample).
- In three months, send a New Member Survey (see sample) to recent members to evaluate their connection and help them get on the path to discipleship.

Reproducibles (see Catch: Program Guide with DVD ROM)

- E-mail Invitation to Coffee With the Pastors
- Follow-Up Letter to Coffee With the Pastors
- Sample Membership Form
- Letter to New Members
- New Member Survey

Step Two: Discipleship Pathway

Evaluate your current discipleship plan for children, youth, and adults. Do you have one? Are you working on reading the entire Bible? Are your children memorizing Scriptures? Do your teens feel like they are growing in faith and knowledge from week to week? Bring together the pastors and education staff and volunteers and talk about what a committed disciple of Jesus Christ looks like, then work backward to determine the path to get there. Be intentional about naming the steps along the way. Our church describes the journey as "Knowing God, Loving God, and Serving God." All of our teaching ministries fall into one or more of these categories. Identify how you want to describe the journey to deeply committed discipleship and communicate the journey and how every class and gathering is a step along the way.

Tasks:

- Gather a meeting of pastors and education staff and volunteers to evaluate your current discipleship model. Create a description of what a deeply committed Christian looks   like and discuss how to offer classes and community opportunities for members to grow on that journey. Use these questions as a guide:

    1. How have you structured your church to help individuals become disciples?

    2. Name your process. Is your process and structure clearly understood by church members?

    3. Name your ministry programs. How are ministry programs moving people toward transformation and making a greater commitment?

    4. How does your overall structure help move a person toward greater levels of commitment?

• Determine how to communicate the discipleship plan to members and help them navigate through class options. Clarify your discipleship process to help individuals get connected within the first six months.

EMAIL INVITATION TO COFFEE WITH THE PASTORS

Attention, Visitors! Join Us for Coffee This Weekend

Are you a visitor to the church? If you are interested in finding out more about our church, or think you might be interested in membership, please join us for Coffee with the Pastors at [date, time, and location]. Childcare is provided.

You'll meet other visitors, find out about the church, and learn what is expected of you if you join. Then, at the end of the coffee, you'll have a chance to formally join the church if you are ready to do so.

Plan to attend Coffee with the Pastors, and then stay for the evening worship service. For more information, go to [Web site] or call [phone number].

FOLLOWUP LETTER TO COFFEE WITH THE PASTORS

Dear _____,

It was a great pleasure to welcome you at Coffee with the Pastors.

What are your next steps on the journey? You may want to consider becoming a member of the church. This commitment will make a world of difference, both in your life and in the lives of the people you will impact through ministry. Our church's staff and connection volunteers are always here to partner with you as you take your next step.

During the Coffee with the Pastors, you learned about our church's four membership expectations:
- Attend worship weekly, unless you are sick or out of town
- Grow in your faith beyond the weekly worship services
- Serve both within and beyond the walls of the church
- Give in proportion to your income, with the tithe being the goal

As we prepare for the upcoming year, we invite you to take the next step forward on your journey by participating in one of our learning communities, which were designed with you in mind. These are a great place to start.

[List learning opportunities and small groups]

May God bless you on your journey!

The United Methodist Church of the Resurrection

MEMBERSHIP FORM

Date _____

Worship Location: Central Campus ☐   Rez West ☐

FAMILY'S PRIMARY ADDRESS

_____

Address   City   State   Zip   Home Phone

HEAD(S) OF HOUSEHOLD JOINING TODAY

Last Name   First   MI

Preferred Name   Date of Birth: Mo/Day/Year

Gender: Male ☐   Female ☐

Marital Status: Single ☐   Couple ☐   Married ☐

Cell Phone   Email

Baptized: Yes ☐ No ☐   Member of another church: Yes ☐ No ☐

Church Name

City   State   Zip

I WANT TO GET INVOLVED

I would like to know more about: (please check)

_____ Alpha   _____ Serving in Missions

_____ Learning Communities   _____ Serving at Resurrection

_____ Group Life   _____ Serving at FaithWork

_____ Children (thru 6th grade)   _____ Support Groups

_____ Students (7-12th grade)   _____ Congregational Care

Other _____

_____

_____

CURRENT INVOLVEMENT (Please list all activities.)

Serving _____

_____

Growing in faith outside of worship _____

_____

_____

HEAD(S) OF HOUSEHOLD JOINING TODAY

Last Name   First   MI

Preferred Name   Date of Birth: Mo/Day/Year

Gender: Male ☐   Female ☐

Marital Status: Single ☐   Couple ☐   Married ☐

Cell Phone   Email

Baptized: Yes ☐ No ☐   Member of another church: Yes ☐ No ☐

Church Name

City   State   Zip

I WANT TO GET INVOLVED

I would like to know more about: (please check)

_____ Alpha   _____ Serving in Missions

_____ Learning Communities   _____ Serving at Resurrection

_____ Group Life   _____ Serving at FaithWork

_____ Children (thru 6th grade)   _____ Support Groups

_____ Students (7-12th grade)   _____ Congregational Care

Other _____

_____

_____

CURRENT INVOLVEMENT (Please list all activities.)

Serving _____

_____

Growing in faith outside of worship _____

_____

_____

continued on reverse

CHILDREN JOINING

Last Name _____ First _____ MI ___

Preferred Name _____

Date of Birth: Mo/Day/Year _____ Gender: Male ☐ Female ☐

Baptized: Yes ☐ No ☐ Confirmed: Yes ☐ No ☐

Last Name _____ First _____ MI ___

Preferred Name _____

Date of Birth: Mo/Day/Year _____ Gender: Male ☐ Female ☐

Baptized: Yes ☐ No ☐ Confirmed: Yes ☐ No ☐

Last Name _____ First _____ MI ___

Preferred Name _____

Date of Birth: Mo/Day/Year _____ Gender: Male ☐ Female ☐

Baptized: Yes ☐ No ☐ Confirmed: Yes ☐ No ☐

Last Name _____ First _____ MI ___

Preferred Name _____

Date of Birth: Mo/Day/Year _____ Gender: Male ☐ Female ☐

Baptized: Yes ☐ No ☐ Confirmed: Yes ☐ No ☐

IMMEDIATE FAMILY MEMBERS NOT JOINING TODAY

Last Name _____ First _____ MI ___

Preferred Name _____

Date of Birth: Mo/Day/Year _____ Gender: Male ☐ Female ☐

Baptized: Yes ☐ No ☐ Confirmed: Yes ☐ No ☐

Last Name _____ First _____ MI ___

Preferred Name _____

Date of Birth: Mo/Day/Year _____ Gender: Male ☐ Female ☐

Baptized: Yes ☐ No ☐ Confirmed: Yes ☐ No ☐

HOW DID YOUR FAMILY LEARN ABOUT RESURRECTION? _____

_____

_____

LETTER TO NEW MEMBERS

Dear _____,

We are delighted to welcome you as a part of our church family. Our prayer is that your faith journey will be one filled with joy!

The purpose of this letter is to share with you some ways to progress toward becoming a "deeply committed Christian," which involves an intentional effort to grow in the areas of knowing, loving, and serving God outside of weekly worship.

For many, a worship service is the first step on this journey of faith. Maybe you've been attending here for two weeks, maybe ten years. Maybe you've already tried a few things; maybe you've just come each week and worshiped quietly. Regardless, there's a simple pathway for the journey of becoming a deeply committed Christian: begin with a learning community, and then commit to a small group. Though it's not the only path you can take, we know from experience that this one works well for many.

You have numerous resources at your immediate disposal. Your first stop is the Connection Point, where team members are on hand before and after worship to connect you with programming or service opportunities. Another option is taking an online mini self-assessment, which you will find at our church Web site.

At Coffee with the Pastors, we learned that membership expectations are:

- Attend worship weekly, unless you are sick or out of town
- Grow in your faith outside of worship, through Bible study and Christian community
- Serve both within and beyond the walls of the church
- Give in proportion to your income, with the tithe being the goal

If you requested information on your membership form about a ministry area, you will soon be contacted. In a few months we'll send you a short survey via email or U.S. mail. We would greatly appreciate your participation in the survey, as it helps us to know how we can improve our service to you.

Again, we are so pleased to have you in our church family!

Blessings to you!

NEW MEMBER SURVEY

Greetings to our newest members!

The purpose of this quick survey is to determine our effectiveness in helping you become a part of our church community. Our main desire is for our members to grow in their journey to know, love, and serve God.

We are committed to being an excellent resource to you as you get started. Thank you for your time!

Name

_____

1. I am currently attending worship
   o   Less than one time per month
   o   One time per month
   o   Two times per month
   o   Three times per month
   o   Four times per month

2. I am growing in faith outside worship
   o   Attending a learning community
   o   Through membership in a small group
   o   Not at this time
   o   Other (please specify)

   _____

3. I am serving / volunteering
   o   Not at this time
   o   This is how I'm serving

   _____

4. I understand that giving is an expression of my faith, with the tithe (10%) being the goal
   o   Yes
   o   No
   o   I want more information on this

5. How were you contacted after you joined the church?
   o   Phone
   o   Email
   o   I was not contacted

6. How do you rate the effectiveness of our current connection efforts?
   - o Poor
   - o Average
   - o Good
   - o Above average
   - o Excellent

7. How could we improve our connection efforts?

_____

8. I would like to be contacted about

_____

9. The best way to contact me is by
   - o Phone _____
   - o Email _____

Thank you for completing this survey!

Appendix:
Documents for Ministries
and Planning

MINISTRY DESCRIPTIONS
AND COMMITMENT FORM

After participating in the *Catch* program, I am compelled to join a ministry team and get to work fishing for people. I understand that Jesus calls us to seek the least and the lost, and that means becoming an outward-focused church. I would like to join the following team:

_____Connection Point Ministry
Learning about church ministries and programs in order to connect visitors and members to them. Staffing the Connection Point desk and directing persons to their desired locations.

_____Mugging Ministry
Regularly delivering mugs / gifts as well as information about the church to first-time visitors. Volunteers will specify their delivery area and pick up mugs from a designated location each week.

_____Traffic Ministry
Perhaps working in conjunction with the trustees or building committee, this group will ensure adequate parking and assistance in the parking lot. In addition, this team will ensure that signage is clear and helpful from the minute a visitor pulls into the parking lot.

_____Marketing / Communications Ministry
This team will ensure that clear, thoughtful, well-designed communication pieces are sent out.

_____Welcoming Worship Ministry
Perhaps in conjunction with the greeters, ushers, and pastoral staff, this team will ensure that persons are greeted at the door, assisted to a seat, and given helpful information. In addition, this team will help make every person in the worship space feel welcomed and invited to participate.

_____Phone Ministry
This team will make cold calls using provided lists, inviting persons to worship as well as to various programs and events throughout the year.

_____Coffee with the Pastors Ministry
This team will work with the pastors to create a welcoming experience in which visitors are encouraged to become members. This may include providing refreshments, setting up or tearing down, and occasionally giving a testimony about being a member of your church.

Name _____

Address _____

Phone _____

Email _____

MY MINISTRY COMMERCIAL

Once you are part of a church ministry, develop a thirty-second "commercial" about it. Your commercial should be a clear, concise, and compelling statement about the work your ministry area does; how that work makes a difference in people's lives; and why someone would want to consider volunteering their time and service to join your efforts. Be prepared to deliver this commercial at any time, so you can take advantage of unexpected, spur-of-the-moment opportunities to invite new people to volunteer with you.

STEP 1
Begin to create your commercial by answering the following questions relating to your ministry:

1. What does my ministry area do, ultimately?

2. How does it make a difference?

3. Why do I enjoy it?

4. What is the best part about the volunteer job I am recruiting for?

5. Why might others enjoy it?

STEP 2
Now, put your commercial together on the lines below using the ideas from your answers above. Add a strong closing question to inspire action. See the example below:

I volunteer for Habitat for Humanity. It's an exciting ministry because it allows me to meet new people and see a tangible difference when I serve. I've also enjoyed learning some new construction techniques. I know you enjoy working on home improvement projects. This would be a great place for you to volunteer. I'm volunteering next Saturday. Why don't you join me?

_____
_____
_____
_____
_____
_____
_____

STEP 3
Practice your delivery. Remember to deliver your commercial with sincerity and enthusiasm. Let the joy you experience in serving shine through!

TRAFFIC MINISTRY

OBJECTIVES

- Serve the Lord
- Support the mission and ministry of the church
- Ensure a safe and positive worship experience
- Optimize the efficiency and safety of traffic flow
- Minimize automobile and pedestrian cross-traffic
- Greet worshipers, volunteers, and staff as they enter and leave facility
- Assist in emergency situations
- Have fun and enjoy the fellowship

HELPFUL TIPS

Wear weather-appropriate clothing.
> Summer – Loose fitting, light materials, sun protection, hat
> Winter – Layers for warmth, including thermal socks, thermal gloves, thermal headwear, thermal face and ear protection
> Spring / fall – Layers that allow you flexibility depending on the changing weather conditions

Wear brightly colored clothing.
> Traffic safety vests and traffic ministry hats will be provided, but the more visible the better.

Wear comfortable, supportive footwear.
> You will be on your feet for an extended duration, so make sure your feet are comfortable.
> If the weather is wet or snowy, ensure that your footwear is waterproof.

When the weather is sunny, wear sunglasses.
> It can get bright out there!

When the weather is rainy, wear a rain suit or poncho.
> Rain ponchos are provided. If you have a rain suit, it will keep you much drier.

When it is dark, wear reflective gear.
> Always carry a flashlight or LED traffic wand.

When you are in close proximity to traffic, be sensitive to your surroundings.
> When you direct cars to stop, make sure they do so before you direct others.

When working pedestrian crossings, manage individuals walking just as you would vehicle traffic.
> Hold the cars for people to walk, and hold the people for cars to pass.
> In inclement weather, give pedestrians priority over vehicles.

When you encounter problems, immediately notify your team leader.
> Problems can range from health issues to situational issues.

Take advantage of breaks.

  Get off your feet, use the restroom, have a snack, warm up or cool down.

  Drink fluids. Hydration is important in both warm and cold weather.

When individuals don't take direction, be courteous.

  Let them go unless it increases the risk for pedestrians or other motorists.

ADDITIONAL COMMENTS

For the most part, everyone will be friendly and appreciative of your efforts. Periodically, however, you will encounter individuals who are angry or upset. The best way to respond is simply to smile and tell them you are a volunteer and are doing your best. If the problem persists, immediately contact your team leader.

If you do not understand the responsibilities of the position you have been assigned, please ask your team leader for clarification before taking the position. If you are not comfortable with the task assigned, please request a change from your team leader.

Have a great time, and remember that the traffic team provides the first impression for visitors when they arrive and the last impression when they leave.

Have fun, and enjoy the fellowship!

GREETER MINISTRY

PURPOSE STATEMENT
To reflect the love of Christ by being welcoming, hospitable, and gracious to those who enter our church home.

MINISTRY SCRIPTURE VERSE
"As God's chosen one, holy and beloved, clothes yourselves with compassion, kindness, humility, meekness and patience" (Colossians 3:12).

GREETER MINISTRY OBJECTIVES

Be faithful to your commitment
Consistency in attendance is vital to this ministry. We can never have too many greeters!

Take ownership
Set the tone. Be relaxed and cheerful in welcoming everyone, including children.

Stay at your assigned door
Direct anyone having questions or needing assistance to the Connection Point, or to one of the worship welcome guides. When giving people directions, never point the way. Always escort them, while being mindful not to leave the door(s) attended.

Display enthusiasm
Your excitement about your church home will make a difference to others.

Generate an atmosphere of care
Warmly receive and welcome everyone. Watch for those who need a hand opening doors or managing babies or young children, especially in inclement weather.

GREETER TEAM TIPS
- Pray before you begin your shift. Be thankful for the blessings of the day, and ask God to shine through you as you represent the church. "And we, who with unveiled faces all reflect the Lord's glory, are being transformed into his likeness with ever-increasing glory, which comes from the Lord, who is the Spirit" (2 Corinthians 3:18).
- Arrive at least thirty minutes prior to the service, and stay until most of the latecomers have arrived.
- Wear your nametag, and collect your greeter badge from the head greeter at the Connection Point before proceeding to your assigned position.
- Please find a substitute if you are not able to keep your scheduled commitment. Keep the roster of your team handy so you can call or email someone to switch weeks with you or take your place.
- If your friends want to stop and talk, please tell them you are "on duty" and you will be happy to catch up with them later.
- Be flexible. Changes will arise, and when they do, remember that you are serving the Lord.

CONNECTION POINT MINISTRY

DESCRIPTION
This team conducts all activities before, during, and after worship services at the Connection Point, the church's information center.

TEAM ACTIVITIES INCLUDE
Consultants are stationed at the Connection Point at each worship service to help integrate members and visitors into the life of our church. Consultants will offer the "20,000-foot view" of all ministries and ministry paths into the church.

Referrals - Consultants will log referrals for subsequent follow-up. These referrals will be related to the ministry area on the Monday following the weekend, using the church database referral system.

Tools - Consultants utilize the following information tools while serving at the Connection Point:
1. Weekly update binder for current team communications and processes
2. Shift notes (located in weekly update binder)
3. Connection Point ministry information binder
4. Ministry index
5. Church Web site
6. Ministry literature
7. Weekly calendar
8. Current volunteer listing
9. Spiritual self-assessment
10. Weekly emails from team leadership with important information on current opportunities
11. Grace for yourself and others! You cannot know everything – no one can. All we can do is our best.

Consultants stay abreast of current connection opportunities within the church and access the computer and / or ministry brochures as needed.

Spiritual mini-assessment - During one-on-one discussion, the consultant may utilize the spiritual self-assessment to help map out ministry options for individuals who visit the Connection Point.

Hospitality duties - Consultants will also perform hospitality duties when needed including: nametag preparation, will-call retrieval, and emergency procedures.

Emergencies - Consultants will be familiar with emergency processes in the event of an emergency situation.

SCHEDULE
Consultants will staff the Connection Point for a minimum of one shift per month before and after worship. Consultants should arrive a half hour before worship and not leave until most worshipers have arrived and worship has begun. Consultants should leave worship shortly before the service is over in order to be at the Connection Point as worshipers exit.

Substitutes - If unable to serve at a shift due to illness, travel, or a personal issue, consultants will find a substitute by personally contacting (a) shiftmates and (b) all teammates, alerting the shift leader about who will be substituting. Consultants will make every effort to find a substitute in advance. Often, shiftmates will trade shifts if contacted in advance. (Note: A phone call to a teammate is often more effective than a "wallpaper" email to all shiftmates.)

Annual / Shift Meetings - Approximately three shift meetings and/or all-team meetings in addition to a Christmas celebration are held each year. Consultants will attend at least one meeting each year (in addition to the Christmas celebration) to get to know their teammates and stay abreast of processes, ministry needs, activities, and other issues.

SPIRITUAL GIFTS AND PERSONALITY STYLES
Extrovert / stable; extrovert / flexible

Spiritual gifts that are typically found in someone serving in this role:
- Administration
- Discernment of spirits
- Exhortation
- Assistance/helps

Passions and skills that are typically found in someone serving in this role:
- Counseling
- Administration skills
- Encouragement of others
- Communication
- Helping / counseling
- Good listening skills
- Hospitality
- Organization
- Spiritual growth
- Christian Community

MUGGING MINISTRY

PURPOSE STATEMENT

To reflect the love of Christ by being welcoming, hospitable, and gracious to those who enter our church home.

MINISTRY SCRIPTURE VERSE

"As God's chosen one, holy and beloved, clothes yourselves with compassion, kindness, humility, meekness and patience" (Colossians 3:12).

MUG DELIVERY TEAM TIPS

When delivering mugs, remember that you are a special representative of the church. Most importantly, you are a representative of Christ!

- Try to deliver the mugs within seventy-two hours after a person's first visit. Mugs can be found at the mug station in the narthex, sorted by zip code.
- A map will be enclosed with each mug to be delivered. If delivering more than one mug, plan your journey ahead of time to take the most direct and efficient route.
- Ring the visitor's doorbell. If the visitor answers, introduce yourself. For example: "My name is_____. I am from _____ and I don't want to come in. I just want to thank you for visiting our church and to give you, as a token of our appreciation, a small gift. (Hand them the mug or gift.) I am glad to answer any questions for you. Again, we just wanted to let you know how much we loved having you in worship, and if you don't have a church home, we wanted you to know it would be an honor for us to be your church family. I hope to see you again soon in worship."
- If they have questions, answer to the best of your knowledge. If you are not sure about something, tell them you will have someone contact them with the answer. After leaving, write a note with the visitor's question, attach it to the map, and return it to the the mug station in the narthex.
- If no one answers the door, jot a quick note to leave with the mug. For example: "Sorry to have missed you. Hope you worship with us again soon! Blessings, (and your name)." Leave the mug on the front porch or in an area where it will be seen when the visitor returns home. If there is a phone number on the map, give the visitor a call to indicate you are sorry you missed them and that you left a mug by the door.
- If delivering to a gated apartment complex, go to the office to see if they will let you in the gate. (If you have the apartment number, most will let you in. If you don't, ask the office personnel if they will please make sure the visitor receives the mug.) Again, if you have a phone number, you can call the visitor to let them know you left a mug at the office.
- The next time you are at church, return the maps to the drop box at the mug station in the narthex. Please note that the names, addresses, and phone numbers provided are to be used for church purposes only. Any violation will be considered an abuse of trust.

Thank you for volunteering your time and making a difference by reaching out through this ministry. "I do it all for the sake of the gospel, that I may share in its blessings" (1 Corinthians 9:23).

PLANNING CALENDAR

Activity	Description	People	Dates

Phase 1. Examination

Activity	Description	People	Dates
Preparation	Invite leadership team	Pastor / leader	
	Order Program Guide with DVD-ROM	Pastor / leader	
	Distribute Program Guide to team • You may photocopy Program Guide • You may email Program Guide file (see DVD-ROM)	Pastor / leader	
Team meetings	Set schedule to read and discuss ideas presented in Program Guide Schedule should include: • Read and discuss "1. Becoming Relentlessly Outward Focused" • Read and discuss "2. Answering Three Important Questions" • Use "Check Point: Looking Inward" to debrief • Read and discuss "3. Attracting People in Your Community" • Read and discuss "4. Making Visitors Feel Welcome" • Read and discuss "5. Connecting and Following Up with Visitors" • Read and discuss "6. Inviting Others to Grow in Faith" • Use "Check Point: Moving Outward" to debrief	Leadership team	
Program planning	Organize teams and activities • Assign leadership of *Catch* teams • Schedule team meetings • Review and plan calendar of activities	Leadership team	

Phase 2. Teaching

Team meetings	Each *Catch* team meets regularly to discuss their plans and activities	*Catch* teams	
	Team leaders meet regularly for check-in and activity updates	Team leaders	

Small-group study	Plan and organize four-week small-group study
	• Set up *Catch* small groups and signup methods
	• Recruit leaders and schedule leader training
	• Determine method for tracking attendance
	• Invite congragation to small groups
	   o Bulletin announcements
	   o Church calendar
	   o Church newsletter
	   o Front page of church Web site
	• Announce start date of small groups
	• Order resources
	   o Small-Group Participant Book for each group member
	   o DVD with Leader Guide for each group
	• Coordinate with worship activities (see below)
		Connection team	

	Carry out four-week small-group study 1. Becoming Relentlessly Outward Focused 2. Answering Three Important Questions 3. Making Visitors Feel Welcome 4. Inviting Others to Grow in Faith	Small groups	
	After Session 4, sign up group members to get involved • Use "Ministry Descriptions and Commitment Form" (see DVD-ROM)		

Worship	Plan worship activities to take place during four-week teaching phase
	• Pastor plan sermons as needed
	• Worship team plan and coordinate other worship activities as needed
	   o Outreach moments
	   o Leadership team reports
	   o Highlight small-group study
		Worship team
		Pastor	

Phase 3. The Launch

Preparation	Reconvene leadership team to plan and stage the launch • Order Implementation Guide • Confirm steps for each team • Set followup meetings to coordinate team activities	Pastor Leadership team	
Marketing	Implement marketing campaign (see Implementation Guide for details) • Evaluate the current marketing effort and message • Plan your direct mail • Create information packets for visitors and materials for the connection center • Plan phone campaigns • Prepare newspaper and radio ads • Equip members to invite visitors	Marketing and Outreach Team	
Worship	Implement worship initiative (see Implementation Guide for details) • Create a Visitor-Friendly Worship Service	Worship Team	
Hospitality	Implement hospitality steps (see Implementation Guide for details) • Invite and train volunteer parking lot greeters • Invite and train a volunteer team of greeters • Encourage members to wear nametags • Create a visitor-friendly worship service • Establish a Connection Center • Establish or improve coffee time • Make room • Care for children • Evaluate phone greeting and voice mail information	Hospitality Team	
Connection	Follow up with visitors (see Implementation Guide for details) • Collect information about visitors • Follow up with first-time visitors • Follow up again after three visits • Be diligent in all connection and follow-up strategies •	Connection Team	
Membership	Facilitate path to membership (see Implementation Guide for details) • Invite returning visitors to join • Discipleship Pathway	Connection Team	